HOW TO USE POCKET HOLE JIG

Joining Materials: Best Practices for Strong Joints

Michael K. Jumper

TABLE OF CONTENTS

INTRODUCTION

In the bustling town of Woodvale, where the sawdust never settled and the hum of power tools filled the air, Emma, a seasoned woodworker, found herself at the local craft fair, her eyes scanning the stalls laden with handmade wonders. However, it wasn't the intricate carvings or the gleaming hardwood tables that caught her attention that day, but a modest book titled "HOW TO USE A POCKET HOLE JIG" displayed at a stall helmed by an old craftsman named Mr. Jacobs.

Emma, curious, approached the stall and picked up the book. Mr. Jacobs, noticing her interest, began to explain its contents with a gentle enthusiasm that only years in the craft could bestow.

"You see, Emma," he started, "this book isn't just about joining pieces of wood. It's about unlocking the full potential of the pocket hole jig — a tool that's as versatile as it is underappreciated."

The book was divided into comprehensive chapters, each detailed in Mr. Jacobs' warm narrative. He shared anecdotes about each technique, like the time he first mastered the angled joints for a custom bookshelf, or the tricks he learned for working with different wood types.

Emma flipped through the pages, each segment offering a clear, step-by-step guide on setting up the jig, adjusting for different woods, and creating joints that were both strong and visually appealing. Photographs and diagrams punctuated the text, providing visual support that was easy to follow.

"What makes this book essential," Mr. Jacobs continued, "is not just the how-to aspect. It's the troubleshooting chapter. It'll save you countless hours and many a headache, I promise you that."

He pointed to a section about common mistakes and how to correct them, a gold mine for both novices and seasoned woodworkers alike. "And it's not just for large projects," he added. "Even something as simple as fixing a wobbly chair or building a sturdy birdhouse can be transformed with the right joinery techniques."

As Emma listened, she realized the value of the book extended beyond the craft itself. It was about efficiency, creativity, and durability in woodworking. Mr. Jacobs spoke of the advanced techniques chapter, detailing how to integrate pocket holes into furniture designs for aesthetic as well as functional benefits.

The final chapter on project ideas was what sealed her decision. It showcased projects ranging from beginner to advanced, each project encouraging practical application of the skills taught in earlier chapters.

"I'll take it," Emma decided, her mind already racing with ideas for her next projects.

As she handed over the payment, Mr. Jacobs smiled. "You're about to make things you never thought you could, with just a simple tool and a bit of know-how. Enjoy the journey, Emma."

Walking away, book in hand, Emma felt inspired. She knew this wasn't just another manual. It was a gateway to mastering a skill that would elevate her woodworking, allowing her to create with confidence and precision. She couldn't wait to get back to her workshop, to start drilling and creating, guided by her new purchase.

CHAPTER 1

Introduction to Your Pocket Hole Jig

Overview of Pocket Hole Joinery

Pocket hole joinery is a popular and effective method used by woodworkers of all skill levels to quickly and efficiently join two pieces of wood together. This technique utilizes a special tool known as a pocket hole jig, which allows for precise drilling of angled holes into one piece of wood. The resulting pocket holes are then used to drive screws into an adjoining piece of wood, creating a strong and durable bond without the need for complex clamps or advanced carpentry skills.

One of the primary advantages of pocket hole joinery is its simplicity. Even beginners can quickly learn how to use a pocket hole jig, making it an excellent starting point for those new to woodworking. The process speeds up many projects, from building cabinets to assembling furniture, because it eliminates many of the more time-consuming steps involved in traditional joinery methods.

The strength of pocket hole joints comes from the angle at which the screw enters the wood. This angle increases the amount of surface area the screw can grip, making the joint incredibly sturdy. Additionally, because the screws act as internal clamps holding the joint together, the need for extensive external clamping is reduced, simplifying the setup and allowing for more rapid assembly.

Another benefit of using pocket hole joinery is the clean appearance it offers. Since all of the screws are inserted at an angle into one piece of wood, the fasteners can often be hidden from view in the final product. This makes pocket hole joinery particularly useful for projects where aesthetics are important, such as in furniture making or cabinetry.

Furthermore, pocket hole joinery is highly versatile. It can be used on a variety of wood types and thicknesses, and it is compatible with multiple join types, including edge-to-edge, edge-to-corner, and edge-to-surface joints. This versatility allows woodworkers to use pocket hole joinery in a wide array of applications, enhancing their ability to tackle different projects and design challenges.

Despite its many benefits, pocket hole joinery is not without its limitations. It is generally not as strong as some traditional joinery methods, such as dovetail or mortise and tenon joints, which can be a consideration for projects that require extremely durable connections. However, for most home woodworking projects and furniture applications, the strength provided by pocket hole joinery is more than sufficient.

Benefits of Using a Pocket Hole Jig

Using a pocket hole jig offers numerous advantages to woodworkers of all skill levels, making it an essential tool in the workshop. One of the primary benefits of this tool is its ability to create strong, reliable joints quickly without requiring complex measurements or intricate joinery techniques. This simplicity accelerates project completion and reduces the learning curve for beginners, while still offering the precision that seasoned craftsmen demand.

The pocket hole jig is especially valued for its versatility. It can be used on a variety of materials ranging from softwoods to hardwoods and even composite materials, making it a universal solution for many woodworking projects. This adaptability ensures that users can move seamlessly between different types of projects without needing to switch tools or techniques.

Another significant advantage of the pocket hole jig is the clean, professional appearance it provides. The joints created with a pocket hole jig are strong and hidden, which enhances the aesthetic of the finished product. This is particularly beneficial for projects where the appearance of the joints is as important as their strength, such as in furniture making and cabinetry.

The tool also allows for quick and easy disassembly, making it ideal for creating furniture that may need to be transported or adjusted in the future. Unlike glued joints, pocket hole joints can be easily unscrewed, allowing for modifications, repairs, or flat-pack furniture designs that can be assembled at a different location.

Moreover, pocket hole joinery doesn't require clamps to hold the joint in place while adhesives dry. These speeds up the workflow because you can continue working on other parts of your project almost immediately after forming the joints. It also reduces the amount of equipment needed, lowering the barrier to entry for new woodworkers and minimizing clutter in the workspace.

Finally, the pocket hole jig is a durable tool that, with proper maintenance, can last for many years. Its design is robust, yet simple, minimizing the possibility of mechanical failures and ensuring that it remains a reliable part of your tool arsenal for a long time.

Essential Tools and Materials

When beginning with a pocket hole jig, it's crucial to have a well-rounded set of tools and materials to ensure successful woodworking projects. The central piece of equipment is the pocket hole jig itself, which comes in various models tailored to different project sizes and complexities. Each jig should be paired with a compatible drill bit, specifically designed to bore the angled holes required for this type of joinery. A drill, preferably a power drill, is necessary to operate the drill bit efficiently.

In addition to the jig and drill, a set of specialized pocket hole screws is essential. These screws are designed with a flat bottom head and a self-tapping tip to fit snugly into the drilled holes, creating strong joints without the need for additional hardware. The length and gauge of the screws will vary depending on the thickness and type of wood being used. It's advisable to have a selection of screws in various sizes to accommodate different materials and joint types.

Clamps are another indispensable tool in the pocket hole joinery process. They hold the pieces of wood firmly in place while drilling and during the assembly process to ensure precise alignment and a clean finish. Face clamps, right angle clamps, and bench clamps are commonly used types, each serving a specific purpose based on the configuration of the workpiece.

A measuring tape and a carpenter's square are fundamental for precise measurements and to ensure that cuts and holes are accurately aligned. Accuracy in measuring and marking workpieces significantly affects the quality and appearance of the final project.

For preparing and finishing the wood, having sandpaper or a power sander is essential. Sanding the edges and surfaces where joints will be made ensures that the finished project is smooth and professional-looking. Additionally, wood glue can be used in conjunction with pocket hole screws to reinforce joints, especially in load-bearing projects or where additional stability is required.

Lastly, safety gear should not be overlooked. Safety glasses protect the eyes from wood shavings and debris, while ear protection is important when using loud power tools. Gloves can provide a better grip and protect hands from splinters and cuts during handling and assembly.

Together, these tools and materials form the foundational setup for anyone looking to explore or perfect their craft in pocket hole joinery. The initial investment in quality tools pays off in the efficiency and strength of the constructed projects, making every woodworking task more enjoyable and successful.

Components of a Pocket Hole Jig

The basic jig is composed of several integral parts that work together to simplify the process of drilling angled holes into wood, making it accessible for both beginners and seasoned craftsmen.

At the core of the pocket hole jig is the drill guide block, typically made from hardened steel to withstand the wear and tear of drilling. This block contains a series of guide holes that are strategically angled to ensure the correct trajectory for the screws. These holes are lined with a special sleeve that helps guide the drill bit smoothly, minimizing friction and preventing damage to the tool and wood.

Attached to the guide block is the alignment base, which serves as the stabilizing platform for the jig. The base is adjustable, allowing users to set the proper height and width for different thicknesses of wood. This ensures that the drill guide block remains securely in place during the drilling process, providing precise and consistent results.

Another essential component is the clamp integrated into the jig, which is used to secure the wood piece while drilling. This clamp may be a simple toggle clamp or a more complex system, depending on the jig model. The clamping mechanism ensures that the wood does not move during the operation, maintaining alignment and safety.

For accurate drilling, pocket hole jigs also include a stop collar that fits around the drill bit. This collar is adjustable and locks in place to control the depth of the drill, ensuring that the screws are neither too shallow nor too deep. Getting the depth right is crucial for the strength of the joint and the appearance of the finished product.

Additionally, most pocket hole jigs come with a selection of drill bits designed specifically for pocket hole joinery. These bits are usually stepped or tiered, allowing them to bore a pilot hole for the screw and a larger clearance hole for the screw head in one operation. The tip of the drill bit is crucial as it determines the size of the pilot hole, which must match the screw size to ensure a tight fit.

Finally, many pocket hole jigs include accessories such as spacers for adjusting the distance between multiple holes, a variety of screws suitable for different types of wood and thicknesses, and sometimes even a carrying case for convenience and portability.

Types of Pocket Hole Jigs

Pocket hole jigs come in a variety of designs, each tailored to different types of woodworking projects and user preferences. The simplest type is the single-hole jig, ideal for beginners or those who only occasionally need to use pocket holes. This compact, portable option is great for small projects and repairs where one or two holes are sufficient.

Moving up in complexity and capability, multi-hole jigs are designed for more frequent use and can handle larger projects. These jigs often feature adjustable parts that can be configured to drill two or more holes in quick succession, speeding up the process when multiple joints are needed. The adjustable settings also allow for greater precision and customization according to the thickness and width of the workpieces.

For professionals or serious woodworking enthusiasts, benchtop pocket hole jigs offer the most features and the best durability. These systems usually include a robust clamp to hold the workpiece securely, a dust collection system to keep the area clean, and preset measurements to facilitate quick and accurate drilling. Benchtop models are particularly beneficial for production settings where efficiency, precision, and repeatability are critical.

Another important consideration is the material from which the jig is made. Basic models might be constructed from plastic, which is lightweight and inexpensive but may not endure heavy or prolonged use. Higher-end models are typically made from metal, providing greater durability and stability, which is crucial for precise, professional-quality work.

The choice of a pocket hole jig also extends to the features it offers, such as built-in storage for bits and accessories, rulers for quick measurement, or the ability to adjust for different angles and thicknesses without additional tools. Some advanced models even feature automation to aid in repetitive tasks, ensuring consistent results every time.

Selecting the right type of pocket hole jig depends on understanding the specific needs of your projects, as well as your budget and how frequently you plan to use the tool. For occasional repairs or small projects, a simple, portable jig might suffice. For more complex or larger scale constructions, investing in a more sophisticated setup will not only increase efficiency but also enhance the strength and quality of the finished product.

How to Choose the Right Jig for Your Project

Choosing the right pocket hole jig for your project is a crucial step that impacts the ease of your work and the quality of your finished product. Different types of pocket hole jigs cater to various needs, ranging from light, occasional use to heavy-duty, professional applications. When selecting a jig, consider factors like the material thickness, the precision required, and your project's scale.

Begin by assessing the scope of your projects. If you're primarily working on small-scale, DIY projects like picture frames or small shelves, a basic pocket hole jig will suffice. These are generally less expensive and easier to handle, making them suitable for hobbyists. For larger projects such as building furniture or cabinetry, a more robust jig that can handle thicker and more varied materials would be a better choice.

Material compatibility is another essential factor. Some jigs are designed to work well with a broad range of wood thicknesses, which is particularly useful if your projects vary significantly. Look for adjustable jigs that allow you to change settings depending on the thickness of the material you're working with. This flexibility helps ensure that the pocket holes are accurately placed, which is vital for the structural integrity of your project.

The ease of use is also a key consideration. Some jigs come with features that make them easier to set up and adjust, such as built-in measuring scales, magnetic clamps, or alignment tools. These features can significantly speed up your workflow and improve accuracy. If you're new to woodworking or pocket hole joinery, choosing a jig with these user-friendly features can make your learning process smoother and more enjoyable.

Durability is critical, especially if you plan to use your jig frequently or for heavy-duty projects. High-quality jigs are typically made from strong materials like steel or aluminum and have robust construction that withstands regular use. Investing in a well-made jig ensures that it remains reliable over time, providing consistent results without needing frequent adjustments or replacements.

Lastly, consider additional accessories and compatibility with other tools. Some jigs can be expanded with accessories like portable bases, clamps, or dust collection attachments, enhancing their versatility. Check whether the jig can integrate with the tools and workspace you already have. This can be a cost-effective way to extend the functionality of your equipment without needing extensive modifications

CHAPTER 2

Setup and Preparation

Assembling Your Pocket Hole Jig

Assembling your pocket hole jig is a straightforward process that requires attention to detail to ensure accuracy and safety in your woodworking projects. Begin by laying out all the components of your jig kit on a clean, flat surface. Typical kits include the jig itself, a drill guide, a clamp, a drill bit, a depth collar, and an Allen wrench.

First, attach the drill guide to the jig base. This is usually done by sliding the guide into a slot or socket on the base until it clicks or locks into place. Make sure the guide is securely fastened to prevent any movement while drilling. Depending on the model of your pocket hole jig, you might also have adjustable settings on the drill guide for different thicknesses of wood. Adjust these settings according to the thickness of the material you will be working with.

Next, insert the drill bit into the chuck of your power drill. Before tightening the chuck, slide the depth collar onto the drill bit. The depth collar controls how deep the drill bit will penetrate into the wood, which is crucial for creating strong, effective joints. Adjust the depth collar according to the thickness of your wood and the screw length you will be using. The collar is usually set by loosening a set screw with the provided Allen wrench, moving the collar to the desired position on the bit, and then retightening the set screw.

After setting up the drill bit and depth collar, secure the jig to your workpiece. If your jig includes a built-in clamp, adjust the clamp to fit the thickness of your workpiece and tighten it to hold the jig firmly in place. For jigs without a built-in clamp, you'll need to use a separate woodworking clamp. Ensure the jig is aligned properly where you want to drill your pocket holes.

Finally, double-check all settings, including the clamp tightness and the depth collar position, before beginning to drill. This ensures that the jig is set up correctly and that you'll produce clean, precise pocket holes that are essential for strong joints

Selecting and Preparing Your Wood

When selecting wood for use with a pocket hole jig, it's essential to consider the type of project and the specific requirements it entails. Hardwoods like oak, maple, and walnut are preferred for their durability and the aesthetic quality they bring to furniture projects. However, they require sharper drill bits and more careful handling to prevent splitting. Softwoods such as pine, cedar, and spruce are easier to work with due to their softer nature, making them ideal for beginners or projects where aesthetics are less critical.

Before beginning any drilling, ensure the wood is in good condition. It should be free of excessive knots, splits, or warping, as these can affect the integrity of the joint and the final result. It's also important to ensure the wood is dry. Moisture can cause the wood to warp or swell, which might affect measurements and the fit of the joint.

Once the appropriate wood is selected, preparation is the next critical step. Begin by cutting the wood to the required dimensions, ensuring each piece is squared and measured accurately. Any inaccuracies in cutting can result in misaligned joints or a finished product that doesn't sit right.

Sanding the edges of the wood where the joints will be made helps to create a cleaner, more professional finish. Removing any rough edges or splinters ensures that the wood pieces fit snugly together and that the surface is smooth for finishing touches after assembly.

Marking the spots where you will drill the pocket holes is vital for precision. Use a pencil and a ruler or a tape measure to make light marks on the wood, indicating where the jig needs to be aligned. This marking ensures that your pocket holes are consistently placed for a uniform appearance and structural integrity.

Finally, once everything is measured and marked, set up your pocket hole jig according to the thickness of your wood and the type of joint you're aiming to create. Adjusting the jig correctly is crucial for ensuring that the screws fit perfectly without protruding through the opposite side of the joint, which can compromise the project's look and strength.

Safety Measures and Best Practices

Safety is paramount when working with any type of power tools, including a pocket hole jig. Ensuring that you follow best practices and adhere to safety measures can prevent accidents and enhance the efficiency and quality of your work.

Before beginning any project, make sure that your work area is well-lit and free of clutter. A tidy workspace reduces the risk of accidents and allows for better control over your materials and tools. Additionally, secure loose clothing and tie back long hair to avoid entanglement in moving parts.

It is crucial to wear the appropriate personal protective equipment. Safety glasses or goggles are essential to protect your eyes from wood chips and dust. For additional safety, consider wearing a face shield when operating the drill. Ear protection is recommended to guard against long-term hearing damage from the noise of drilling, especially during extended periods of work. Dust masks or respirators should be worn to prevent inhalation of sawdust, particularly when working with materials like MDF, which can contain harmful adhesives.

Inspect your pocket hole jig and all related tools before use. Check the jig for any damage or loose components, and ensure that all adjustments and settings are correct for your workpiece to prevent the tool from slipping or misaligning.

Verify that the drill bit is sharp and free from damage as a dull bit can lead to inaccurate drilling and increased risk of kickback.

Properly setting up the jig involves adjusting the drill guide based on the thickness of the wood. This ensures that the pocket holes are drilled at the correct angle and depth, which is critical for creating strong, reliable joints. Always use the stop collar on the drill bit to control the depth of the hole and prevent drilling too deeply into the material.

When positioning the wood and jig, make sure the wood is securely clamped. This not only prevents the wood from moving as you drill but also keeps your hands free and clear of the drill bit. Never attempt to hold the workpiece by hand while drilling, as this can lead to serious injuries.

It's important to let the drill do the work. Applying too much force can cause the drill bit to break or the wood to split. Keep the drill at full speed before making contact with the wood and maintain steady pressure to ensure clean, smooth holes.

After drilling, take the time to clean up any debris and sawdust from the work area and your tools. This not only maintains a safe workspace but also prolongs the life of your tools and equipment.

Finally, regularly review safety guidelines related to the use of drills and pocket hole jigs. Staying informed about safe practices and the potential hazards of woodworking will help you undertake projects with confidence and care, ensuring a safe and enjoyable experience every time.

CHAPTER 3

Measurements and Adjustments

Setting the Drill Guide

Setting the drill guide correctly is a critical step in using a pocket hole jig effectively. This ensures that the holes are drilled at the optimal angle and depth for strong, reliable joints. The drill guide, which is part of the pocket hole jig, determines the trajectory of the drill bit. Proper adjustment of this component is crucial for various wood thicknesses and types.

To begin, identify the thickness of the wood you are working with. Most pocket hole jigs come with markings that correspond to common thicknesses like 1/2 inch, 3/4 inch, and 1 inch. Align the edge of the drill guide with the marking that matches your wood's thickness. This alignment is essential as it dictates the angle and depth at which the drill bit enters the wood, ensuring the screw securely joins the pieces without splitting the wood.

Next, adjust the depth collar on the drill bit. This collar controls how deep the bit will drill into the wood. Place the drill bit into the guide and hold it against the wood. The tip of the bit should just touch the bottom of the wood piece. Tighten the set screw on the collar once it is in the correct position. This step is vital to prevent the drill from going too deep, which could weaken the joint or cause the screw to protrude from the opposite side.

For different wood types, consider the density of the material. Softer woods may require slightly shallower depths to avoid splitting, while harder woods can handle deeper screws for a stronger hold. Some jigs feature adjustable angles, which can be tailored according to the specific requirements of the project. For example, a steeper angle may be necessary for very thick woods or when working near the edge of a board to prevent breakout.

It's also advisable to use a test piece of wood before drilling into your final workpiece. This allows you to verify the settings and make any necessary adjustments without compromising your project. Once you are satisfied with the setup on your test piece, replicate the settings on your actual workpiece.

Remember to keep the jig firmly clamped during drilling to maintain precision. Any movement could alter the trajectory of the hole, leading to a weaker joint. After drilling, check the holes to ensure they are clean and to the correct depth. Adjustments should be minor and incremental to hone in on the perfect setup.

By carefully setting the drill guide and adjusting the depth collar, you optimize the effectiveness of your pocket hole jig. This preparation not only enhances the strength of the joints but also contributes to the overall finish and durability of your woodworking projects.

Adjusting the Drill Bit Depth

Adjusting the drill bit depth is crucial when using a pocket hole jig because it determines the angle and depth of the screw placement, ensuring the screw securely joins the two pieces of wood without causing damage. The first step in this process is to select the correct drill bit for the screw size you plan to use, which is usually included in the jig kit.

Once the appropriate drill bit is selected, you must set the depth collar on the drill bit. This collar controls how deep the drill bit can penetrate into the wood. The depth should be set so that the tip of the screw will emerge at the midpoint of the joined piece's thickness. This placement provides the strongest hold and reduces the risk of the wood splitting.

To set the depth collar, place the drill bit next to the jig's depth-setting gauge, which is often built into the jig itself. Align the tip of the drill bit with the corresponding mark on the gauge that matches the thickness of the wood you are working with. For example, if you are drilling into 3/4 inch thick wood, align the tip of the drill bit with the 3/4 inch marking on the gauge.

After aligning the drill bit, slide the depth collar along the bit until it rests against the top of the gauge. This will be your stopping point when drilling. Tighten the set screw on the depth collar using an Allen wrench or the built-in hex key to secure it in place. It's important to ensure the collar is tightened properly to prevent it from moving while drilling, which could lead to holes of incorrect depth.

Before starting your project, it's a good idea to test the setup on a scrap piece of wood of the same thickness as your project material. Drill a pocket hole and then drive a screw into the hole. Check that the tip of the screw fits snugly into the middle of the thickness of the second piece of wood, without poking through or stopping too short.

Remember, different wood densities might require slight adjustments in the depth setting. Softer woods may allow the screw to drive deeper easily, while harder woods might resist screw penetration, necessitating a slightly shallower depth setting.

Choosing the Right Screws for the Material Thickness

When using a pocket hole jig, one of the most critical factors for ensuring strong and durable joints is selecting the appropriate screws for the material thickness. This choice affects not only the strength of the finished joint but also its appearance and structural integrity over time.

The general rule for choosing the right screws is that the length of the screw should be approximately 1.5 times the thickness of the material being joined. For example, if you are working with ¾-inch thick wood, the ideal screw length would be 1 ¼ inches. This guideline ensures that the screw is long enough to penetrate and hold the adjoining piece securely without poking through the opposite side.

Different types of screws are designed for specific materials and applications. For most indoor projects involving softwoods or plywood, fine-threaded screws are preferable because they provide better grip and strength. However, for harder woods, coarse-threaded screws are recommended as they are easier to drive into dense materials and reduce the likelihood of the wood splitting.

When joining thinner or more delicate materials, it's important to choose screws with a smaller diameter to prevent damaging the wood. Conversely, for thicker and heavier materials, larger screws may be necessary to maintain joint strength. The head of the screw also plays a vital role; a larger head provides more surface area, enhancing the screw's ability to hold the joint together under stress.

Materials like MDF or particleboard require special consideration. These materials are less dense and can be prone to splitting or crumbling under pressure. Therefore, using screws specifically designed for such materials, which often have a wider thread pitch and are made from stronger metals, can prevent damage and improve the joint's durability.

It's also important to consider the finish and corrosion resistance of the screws, especially for projects that will be exposed to moisture or outdoor conditions. Stainless steel or coated screws resist rust and corrosion better than ordinary steel screws, making them ideal for outdoor furniture, decks, and other exterior projects.

Lastly, while selecting the right screw length and type is essential, setting the correct drill bit depth on the pocket hole jig is equally important. The drill bit depth should be adjusted according to the thickness of the material to ensure the screw sits flush with or slightly below the surface of the wood. This adjustment prevents the material from splitting when the screw is driven in and ensures a clean, professional finish on the final product.

CHAPTER 4

Drilling Pocket Holes

Step-by-Step Drilling Process

Begin by ensuring that your pocket hole jig is firmly secured to your workbench or a stable surface to prevent any movement during the drilling process. Select the appropriate drill bit for the thickness of the wood you are working with. Most pocket hole jigs come with a chart that helps you determine the correct settings based on the thickness of your material.

Adjust the jig settings according to the thickness of your workpiece. This typically involves setting the depth collar on the drill bit to match the thickness of your material. The depth collar controls how deep the drill bit will penetrate into the wood, ensuring that the pocket hole is neither too shallow nor too deep. Secure the depth collar with the provided set screw once it is in the correct position.

Place the wood into the jig, making sure it is flush against the jig's stops. If your jig has adjustable stops, you may need to set these based on the width of your material. Clamp the wood securely in place. A strong clamp prevents the wood from moving as you drill and ensures accurate hole placement.

Insert the drill bit into your drill/driver. Begin drilling at a moderate speed to prevent the wood from splintering. As you drill, apply steady pressure to drive the bit through the wood and into the jig. The drill should easily pull itself into the wood without requiring excessive force.

As the drill bit reaches the depth set by the collar, you will feel a decrease in resistance, signaling that the correct depth has been achieved. Withdraw the drill slowly to clear the wood chips from the hole. Avoid pulling out too quickly, which can cause splintering around the entry of the hole.

After drilling the first hole, if your project requires multiple pocket holes, reposition the wood in the jig according to your measurement marks and repeat the drilling process for each subsequent hole. Ensure that each hole is spaced properly according to your project's requirements.

Once all holes are drilled, remove the wood from the jig and prepare for the next step of your project, typically involving joining the drilled pieces using pocket screws. Insert the screws through the pocket holes and into the adjoining piece of wood. It's important to use a screw length appropriate for the thickness of the wood to ensure a tight, secure joint.

Clean any wood chips or debris from your jig and work area to maintain a safe and efficient workspace. Proper maintenance of your tools, including regular cleaning and inspection, will prolong their life and ensure accurate and reliable results in your woodworking projects.

Tips for Clean and Efficient Drilling

Drilling clean and efficient pocket holes is crucial for creating strong, invisible joints in woodworking projects. To achieve this, start by ensuring your pocket hole jig and drill bits are clean and free from debris. Wood chips and sawdust can interfere with the jig's accuracy and the drill bit's efficiency.

Selecting the correct drill bit size for the screw and material thickness is essential. Most pocket hole jigs come with a chart that helps you match the screw length and drill bit size with the thickness of your wood. Using the right settings prevents the wood from splitting and ensures the screws sit flush with or below the surface of the wood.

Before drilling, secure the wood piece firmly. A sturdy clamp or vise will prevent the wood from moving, which can cause the holes to be misaligned or the wood to splinter. Position the jig precisely where you want the joint to ensure the drill enters the wood at the correct angle.

When you start drilling, maintain a steady, moderate speed to allow the drill bit to cut cleanly through the wood. Drilling too fast can generate excessive heat, which dulls the drill bit and burns the wood. On the other hand, drilling too slowly can make the process inefficient and may not provide clean cuts.

Use a sharp drill bit to achieve cleaner holes. A dull bit can tear the wood fibers instead of cutting them, resulting in rough edges that could weaken the joint. Check and replace your drill bits regularly to maintain the best performance.

As you drill each hole, periodically clear out the wood chips and debris. This not only keeps the work area clean but also reduces the friction and heat build-up, which can negatively affect the drill bit's life and the quality of the hole. Some drill bits are designed with flutes that help eject the debris as you drill, aiding in cleaner and more efficient drilling.

After drilling, inspect the holes for any irregularities. If the edges are rough, lightly sand them or use a small file to smooth them out. This prevents the wood from splitting when you insert the screws and results in a stronger, more aesthetic joint.

Finally, applying a small amount of lubricant to the drill bit can help reduce heat and friction during drilling. This practice is particularly useful in hardwoods, which are denser and can cause more wear on your drill bits.

Avoiding Common Drilling Mistakes

When drilling pocket holes using a pocket hole jig, there are several common mistakes that can affect the quality and strength of your joints. Recognizing and avoiding these errors can significantly enhance your woodworking projects.

One frequent error is not setting the drill bit to the correct depth. This mistake can lead to screws that don't sit flush with or penetrate through the workpiece. To avoid this, always ensure that the drill bit collar is adjusted according to the thickness of your wood. Use the measurements provided on the jig or refer to the jig's manual to set the correct depth.

Improper placement of the pocket hole is another common issue. Placing holes too close to the edge of the wood can cause it to split, while placing them too far might weaken the joint. Generally, the pocket hole should be centered 3/4 inch from the edge of the workpiece. For thinner or thicker materials, adjust the placement accordingly, keeping structural integrity in mind.

Choosing the wrong screw size can also compromise the joint. Screws that are too long can poke out the opposite side of the joint, while too short screws may not hold securely. Check the jig's guidelines for the appropriate screw length, which usually depends on the thickness of the wood.

Over-tightening the screws is a common mistake that can strip the pocket hole or crack the wood. This is especially true with softer woods. To prevent this, use a drill with a clutch setting that stops when a certain resistance is met, ensuring that the screw is tight but not overtightened.

Failing to secure the workpieces properly before drilling can lead to misaligned holes. Always clamp the jig firmly to your workpiece and maintain a stable working surface to ensure accurate drilling.

Inconsistent drilling speed and pressure can result in rough, uneven holes that weaken the joint. Maintain a steady, moderate speed when drilling, allowing the drill bit to cut through the wood without forcing it. This results in cleaner holes and stronger joints.

Using a dull or damaged drill bit can tear the wood fibers around the pocket hole, leading to a weak joint. Regularly inspect and replace your drill bits to ensure clean, sharp cuts. If the wood burns while drilling, it's a clear sign that the bit is dull and needs replacing.

Not clearing wood chips from the jig can obstruct subsequent holes and affect the precision of the drill. Always clear the chips after drilling each hole to keep the area clean and ensure that the drill bit aligns correctly for the next hole.

CHAPTER 5

Creating Strong Joints

Types of Joints You Can Make with a Pocket Hole Jig

Pocket hole joinery is celebrated for its versatility and strength, making it a favorite among woodworking enthusiasts for constructing everything from furniture to custom cabinetry. Utilizing a pocket hole jig, woodworkers can effortlessly create several types of strong, reliable joints tailored to the specific needs of their projects.

One of the most basic and frequently used joint is the butt joint, where the end of one piece of wood is attached to the face of another. This type of joint is ideal for simple constructions like frames or boxes. The pocket holes are drilled at an angle into one end of the wood, and then screws are driven into the adjoining piece, pulling the two tightly together. The angle of the pocket hole provides ample clamping force and makes the joint easy to assemble.

Edge joining is another popular technique enabled by pocket hole jigs. This method is used to join two pieces of wood along their edges to form a larger panel, such as for tabletops or door panels. By drilling pocket holes along the edge of one piece and screwing it into the adjacent piece, woodworkers can create a seamless and strong joint that is also aesthetically pleasing because the screws are hidden on the underside.

Miter joints, typically used for picture frames or decorative trims, involve joining two pieces of wood at an angle, commonly 45 degrees. Pocket hole joinery can strengthen miter joints significantly. By placing pocket holes on the inside of the miter cut, the screws pull the joint together tightly, which is especially beneficial in applications where the joint is subjected to tension or pulling forces.

Another functional joint achievable with a pocket hole jig is the T-joint, which is used when one piece of wood needs to be joined to the middle of another piece, such as attaching shelves to a cabinet side or building partitions. Pocket holes make these joints easy to assemble and strong enough to handle considerable weight.

For more complex furniture designs, corner joints are essential, and pocket hole joinery provides a simple yet strong solution for joining pieces at a 90-degree angle. This is particularly useful in box construction and cabinetry where the integrity of the joint impacts the overall stability of the piece.

Finally, the frame joint, a variant of the corner joint, is used in constructing larger frames and bases of items like tables and beds. Pocket holes allow for quick assembly and robust joints that can withstand heavy loads, even when the joint itself is not visible in the final product.

Techniques for Aligning Joints

Creating strong joints with a pocket hole jig requires precision and care, especially when it comes to aligning the pieces of wood to be joined. Proper alignment is critical because it affects the strength, appearance, and structural integrity of the final product. To achieve perfect alignment, there are several techniques and considerations that woodworkers should keep in mind.

The first step in ensuring accurate joint alignment with a pocket hole jig is to mark the locations where the pocket holes will be drilled. Use a pencil and a ruler to make clear, precise marks, ensuring that each mark corresponds exactly to where the joint will be positioned. This prevents any misalignment due to guesswork during the drilling process.

Once the marks are made, setting up the pocket hole jig correctly is essential. Adjust the jig according to the thickness of the wood pieces being joined. Most pocket hole jigs have settings that allow for adjustments to accommodate various wood thicknesses. This ensures that the pocket holes are drilled at the correct angle and depth, providing optimal grip and strength in the joint.

Clamping the wood securely is another crucial step. Use clamps to hold the wood pieces firmly in place on the workbench, ensuring that they do not move during the drilling process. This not only helps in maintaining alignment but also prevents the wood from splitting or the drill bit from slipping, which could lead to inaccurate holes.

When it comes time to join the pieces, applying the right amount of glue can make a difference. Spread a thin layer of wood glue on the joining surfaces before screwing them together. The glue helps to fill any minor gaps between the wood pieces, enhancing the strength of the joint.

After applying glue, align the pieces based on the marks previously made and use clamps again to hold the pieces together. This step is critical as it keeps the wood in place while the screws are being driven in. Drive the screws through the pocket holes into the adjoining piece of wood at a steady pace, making sure not to overtighten as this could strip the wood and weaken the joint.

For large projects or when joining heavier pieces of wood, consider using additional support mechanisms along with the pocket hole jig. Right-angle clamps or dowels can be used to reinforce the joint, providing extra stability and ensuring that the alignment holds over time.

Finally, always check the alignment as you progress, especially before the glue sets. Small adjustments can be made before the glue dries to ensure that the final product looks good and functions well. This may involve loosening and re-tightening screws, applying additional pressure with clamps, or even redrilling a pocket hole if necessary.

Clamping Strategies for Secure Joinery

When using a pocket hole jig to create wood joints, one of the most critical steps to ensure strong and durable connections is proper clamping. Clamping holds the pieces of wood firmly in place during the drilling and screwing process, preventing movement that could lead to misalignment or weakened joints.

The choice of clamp depends on the specific project and the size of the wood pieces being joined. For most pocket hole projects, a right-angle clamp is invaluable because it helps to maintain the right angle between two pieces while screwing them together. This type of clamp typically has one arm that fits inside the pocket hole, holding the screw in place and pushing against the adjoining piece of wood, thereby pulling the joint tightly together.

Another effective clamping strategy involves using face clamps. These clamps apply pressure across the joint line from the outside, ensuring that the surfaces are flush and tight against each other. Face clamps are particularly useful for larger pieces where alignment is crucial and where additional support is needed to maintain surface contact while the screws are driven in.

For larger assemblies or when working with several joints at once, bar clamps or pipe clamps can be used. These clamps provide a wider reach and can apply consistent pressure across multiple joints, making them ideal for constructing larger pieces like tables or shelves. It's important to periodically check the alignment as you tighten the clamps to avoid any shifting of the wood pieces.

In cases where the woodworking project involves curved or irregularly shaped pieces, specialty clamps, such as band clamps or strap clamps, may be necessary. These clamps can wrap around the entire assembly and apply even pressure in a circular or irregular pattern, which is essential for maintaining joint integrity in non-linear designs.

Regardless of the type of clamp used, it's essential to use a protective layer between the clamp and the wood to prevent damage to the wood surface. Soft pads or scraps of wood can serve as a buffer, protecting the wood from imprints or dents from the clamp's pressure.

To further enhance joint strength, it is advisable to clean up any excess glue that squeezes out from the joint immediately after clamping and before it sets. This not only ensures a clean finish but also prevents the glue from interfering with the wood's expansion and contraction, which can impact the longevity and durability of the joint.

Timing also plays a crucial role in clamping. Once the pieces are positioned and the screws are driven in, they should remain clamped until the glue has fully cured, according to the manufacturer's instructions. This duration will ensure that the joint is as strong as possible.

CHAPTER 6

Working with Different Materials

Using a Pocket Hole Jig with Hardwoods

Hardwoods, with their dense grain structure and aesthetic appeal, are often the preferred choice for premium furniture and cabinetry. Working with these materials using a pocket hole jig requires some specific considerations to ensure strong, clean joints that are both functional and visually pleasing.

When drilling pocket holes in hardwoods such as oak, maple, or walnut, selecting the correct drill bit is crucial. Typically, a stepped drill bit specifically designed for hardwood use is recommended because it can handle the material's hardness without causing burning or premature wear. The drill speed should be adjusted to a lower setting compared to softer woods to prevent the bit from overheating.

The depth setting on the pocket hole jig also needs careful adjustment. Hardwoods require the drill bit to penetrate at a controlled depth to avoid cracking the wood. This is especially important near the ends and edges of the board. Make sure the depth stop on the drill bit is set so that the tip just exits the opposite side of the board. This ensures the screw has enough wood to grip without blowing out the side or splitting the wood.

Choosing the right screws is another critical factor. Fine-threaded screws are generally better for hardwoods because they provide a stronger hold without splitting the wood. The length of the screw should be appropriate for the thickness of the materials being joined; typically, a screw that is at least 1 inch longer than the thickness of the material will provide a secure joint.

Before driving the screws, it is advisable to apply a small amount of lubricant on the threads to reduce friction and prevent the wood from cracking. Additionally, clamping the workpieces firmly together before screwing will prevent the pieces from shifting and will help achieve a flush, tight joint.

Pre-drilling pilot holes at the screw exit points can also be beneficial in preventing wood splitting, especially when working near the edge of a board. This step, while not always necessary, can be crucial for maintaining the integrity of the joint and the finish of the project.

For finish work, any pocket holes that will be visible in the final project should be filled with wooden plugs that match the wood type and grain. These plugs can be glued in place, trimmed flush, and then sanded to blend seamlessly with the surrounding surface, thus maintaining the aesthetic qualities of the hardwood.

Finally, regular maintenance of the pocket hole jig and its components is essential when working with hardwoods. The increased wear from the dense materials can lead to dulling of the drill bit and other components, which in turn can affect the quality of the joints. Regularly check and replace these parts as needed to keep the tool performing at its best.

Using a Pocket Hole Jig with Softwoods

Softwoods, characterized by their lighter weight and ease of manipulation, are commonly used in woodworking projects ranging from furniture to decorative items. When using a pocket hole jig with softwoods like pine, cedar, or spruce, it's crucial to take certain precautions and adjustments to ensure strong, effective joints without damaging the material.

One of the primary considerations when working with softwoods is the setting of the drill bit depth. Because softwoods are less dense than hardwoods, setting the depth too deep can lead to breakthroughs or weakened joints where the screw might strip the wood. To avoid this, adjust the depth setting on your pocket hole jig slightly shallower than you would for hardwoods. This adjustment ensures that the screws grip securely without stressing the wood excessively.

Choosing the right screws is another vital step. For softwoods, use fine-threaded screws which are specifically designed to grip better in less dense materials. These screws ensure a tighter hold and reduce the likelihood of splitting the wood, which is a common issue due to the softer nature of these woods.

Pre-drilling is especially important in softwoods to prevent splitting. Even though a pocket hole jig eliminates the need for drilling pilot holes in many scenarios, in very soft or thin pieces, pilot holes can add an extra layer of security. When drilling, maintain a steady, moderate speed to avoid overheating, which can cause the wood fibers around the screw to weaken.

Clamping is another critical step that can't be overlooked. Softwoods are susceptible to shifting during the screwing process, so a firm clamp is necessary to hold the pieces in place. This ensures that the alignment doesn't change as the screws are driven in, which could otherwise compromise the precision of the joint.

Finally, consider the overall handling of softwoods during the project. These materials can dent and scratch more easily than hardwoods, so gentle handling and proper storage of the wood before use will keep it in the best condition for your project.

Considerations for Composite and Plywood

When working with composite materials and plywood using a pocket hole jig, several factors must be considered to ensure successful joints and maintain the integrity of the materials. Composite materials, such as MDF or particle board, are dense and can be prone to splitting when not handled correctly. To mitigate this, it's essential to use a fine-thread screw specifically designed for these materials, which grips better without causing damage.

Plywood, on the other hand, presents a different challenge due to its layered structure. When drilling into plywood, there is a risk of delamination where the layers of the wood could separate. To prevent this, it is advisable to place the pocket holes along the edges of the plywood where there is less likelihood of impacting the layered structure directly. Additionally, using a slightly lower torque setting on your drill can prevent the screw from being overdriven, which could otherwise lead to splitting at the hole site.

Both composite materials and plywood benefit from using a backing board under the piece being drilled. This not only supports the material during the drilling process but also helps to minimize tear-out on the backside of the piece as the drill exits the material. Ensuring that the drill bit is sharp and clean is crucial for both types of materials. A dull bit can create excessive heat and friction, which not only affects the quality of the hole but can also damage the material.

Spacing the pocket holes appropriately is important in preventing the material from weakening. In composite materials, holes should be spaced slightly further apart compared to solid wood, as composites are less dense and more prone to cracking under stress. For plywood, ensuring that the holes are not too close to the edge of the material can help maintain the structural integrity of the plywood, reducing the risk of the edges splitting.

When assembling, applying a suitable adhesive in conjunction with the screws can add significant strength to the joint. This is especially beneficial in plywood to help counteract the potential for the layers to separate over time. In composites, the glue helps to distribute the load across a larger area, reducing stress at the screw points.

Finally, it is vital to adjust the clamp pressure when holding the material during drilling and assembly. Excessive pressure can cause composites and plywood to deform or crack, particularly around the pocket holes. Gentle, even pressure ensures that the material remains flat and stable while forming the joint.

CHAPTER 7

Advanced Joinery Techniques

Creating Angled Joints

Creating angled joints using a pocket hole jig is an advanced technique that allows woodworkers to join pieces at various angles, typically ranging from 90 degrees to less acute angles like 45 degrees. This capability is especially useful for projects involving complex shapes and structures, such as frames, cabinets, and various types of furniture.

To begin, the correct setup of the pocket hole jig is crucial. The jig needs to be adjusted according to the thickness of the wood and the angle at which the joint is required. Most pocket hole jigs come with an adjustable guide that helps in setting the angle for the drill bit. It's important to ensure that the drill guide is set at the correct angle so that the pocket holes are accurately positioned for the specific joint configuration.

When drilling into angled pieces, securing the workpiece is essential to prevent movement and ensure precision. Using clamps can stabilize the wood during the drilling process. It is advisable to use a clamp that is compatible with the jig to hold the wood in place tightly. For angled joints, sometimes a custom setup or jig accessory is required to hold the piece at the right angle securely.

Choosing the right screw length is another critical factor. The screw must be long enough to bridge the gap and bite into the joining piece effectively without protruding through the opposite side. Screws that are too short will not hold the joint securely, while screws that are too long can damage the wood or compromise the joint's aesthetics.

Once the pocket holes are drilled, aligning the pieces to be joined involves careful placement and additional clamping. Special attention should be paid to how the pieces fit together to ensure that the angle is maintained throughout the joining process. A good practice is to dry-fit the pieces before final assembly to check for any adjustments needed in the alignment or screw length.

During assembly, applying a small amount of wood glue can enhance the strength of the joint, although it's not strictly necessary since the mechanical strength provided by the screws is usually sufficient. However, glue can help in creating a more seamless appearance and add to the durability of the joint.

After the pieces are joined, filling the pocket holes with wood plugs or filler can provide a smooth, finished look. This step is especially important in projects where the aesthetics of the joint are as important as its structural integrity.

Maintaining the jig and drill bits is important to ensure clean cuts and accurate joints over time. Regularly cleaning the jig, checking for wear on the guide holes, and sharpening or replacing the drill bits can help achieve the best results with every project.

Working with Curved and Complex Shapes

Working with curved and complex shapes using a pocket hole jig can be a rewarding challenge, demanding precision and creativity. When joining these types of shapes, it's crucial to understand that the success of the joint hinges on the accuracy of the pocket hole placement and the selection of the appropriate screws.

The first step in working with curves or irregular shapes is to accurately mark where the pocket holes should be drilled. This often involves creating a template from scrap material that mirrors the curvature or complexity of the piece being joined. By affixing the template to the workpiece, you can ensure that the drill guide aligns correctly, maintaining the angle and depth consistency essential for strong joints.

Selecting the right screws is paramount. For curved and complex shapes, using a shorter screw can sometimes be beneficial as it helps prevent the tip from exiting the curved surface. The screw length and the drill bit settings must be carefully adjusted based on the thickness and density of the wood to avoid compromising the integrity of the joint.

Clamping is another critical aspect. Curved and complex shapes require specialized clamps that can conform to the shape and hold the pieces firmly in place during drilling and screwing. Spring clamps or adjustable band clamps often work well for these applications because they distribute pressure evenly and can adapt to various profiles.

When drilling into curved or complex shapes, it's important to maintain a steady hand and ensure that the drill is perpendicular to the surface to prevent the pocket holes from being misaligned. A common technique is to use a drill press with a jig setup that holds the workpiece steady, although many experienced woodworkers develop the skill to drill these holes freehand with a portable drill.

After drilling the pocket holes, the next challenge is aligning the pieces to be joined. This often requires careful positioning and sometimes the use of additional support structures or temporary joints to hold the assembly in the desired shape while the screws are inserted.

The flexibility of a pocket hole jig comes into play with the ability to make adjustments on the fly. For example, if a joint isn't as tight as it should be, you can often reposition the pocket hole slightly or use a slightly larger screw to achieve a tighter fit.

Finally, when working with complex or curved shapes, finishing becomes critically important. The holes should be filled with wood plugs or filler that matches the wood type and grain. Sanding the joints until they are smooth and flush with the surface ensures that the final product looks seamless and professionally crafted.

Integrating Pocket Holes in Furniture Making

Pocket hole joinery is a revered technique among woodworkers for its strength and simplicity, particularly in furniture making where durability and aesthetics are paramount. The method involves driving self-tapping screws into angled holes drilled into the wood. This creates a secure and hidden joint, perfect for a variety of applications from building cabinets to crafting custom tables.

One of the first considerations when integrating pocket holes into furniture making is the selection of the correct jig setting and screw length. This depends largely on the thickness of the wood. Typically, a pocket hole jig can be adjusted to accommodate different wood thicknesses, ensuring that the pocket hole screws are positioned optimally for maximum joint strength without breaking through the other side of the workpiece.

The placement of pocket holes is critical and should be planned according to the project design. For instance, when constructing a cabinet, pocket holes can be placed on the inside of the cabinet pieces to ensure that they remain hidden from view once assembled. It's also beneficial to use a clamp when drilling and driving screws to keep the wood pieces aligned and prevent shifting, which could compromise the joint's integrity.

Another advanced technique in furniture making with pocket holes involves creating angled joints, such as those needed for chairs or picture frames. Special clamps and jig accessories are available to hold the pieces at the appropriate angle while drilling and fastening. This allows for strong angled connections that are difficult to achieve with other types of joinery.

When designing furniture that will bear significant load, such as beds or large dining tables, reinforcing pocket hole joints with additional hardware or adhesive can enhance durability. Although pocket holes provide substantial strength on their own, areas subjected to excessive stress can benefit from the added security of these reinforcements.

For aesthetic purposes, pocket holes should be strategically placed to remain unseen or easily covered with wood plugs that match the project's finish. After constructing the joint, filling the holes with wooden plugs, sanding down the surface, and applying the finish can virtually hide the fasteners, maintaining the seamless appearance of the furniture.

CHAPTER 8

Troubleshooting

Common Issues and How to Solve Them

When using a pocket hole jig, one common issue is the misalignment of the drill bit, which can lead to imperfect holes. To solve this, always ensure the jig is securely clamped to the workpiece and that the drill bit is correctly seated in the guide. Check that your drill is set to the appropriate speed; too fast can lead to overheating and too slow may not penetrate properly.

Another frequent problem is wood splitting, particularly with softer woods or near the edge of a workpiece. To prevent this, position your pocket holes at least ¾ inch from the edge of the wood. Also, consider using finer-threaded screws designed for softwood. Pre-drilling pilot holes can also help reduce splitting in brittle woods.

Sometimes the screws do not sit flush with or sink below the surface of the wood, which can affect the aesthetics and structural integrity of the project. This can be caused by using the incorrect screw length. Double-check that the screw length matches the thickness of your wood. If the settings are correct but the problem persists, ensure the drill bit is sharp and not worn out.

The jig itself can become worn over time, especially the drill guides, which can lead to inaccurate drilling. Regularly inspect the jig for any signs of wear or damage. If the guides are worn out, they should be replaced. Keeping your jig clean and free of sawdust and debris also ensures more accurate placements.

In some cases, the wood may burn as you drill. This burning is typically due to either a dull drill bit or excessive speed. Always use sharp drill bits and adjust the drill speed based on the hardness of the wood. For harder woods, slower speeds help prevent burning and ensure cleaner cuts.

Occasionally, the joint may end up weaker than expected. This could be due to not using enough screws or the screws being too small. Ensure you're using the recommended number of screws for the joint size, and consider using larger screws or adding more screws to distribute the load more evenly.

Lastly, if you find that removing or adjusting screws is difficult, it might be because the screw heads are stripped or the driver bit is not the correct fit. Use a bit that fits snugly into the screw head, and replace bits that show signs of wear. If a screw head gets stripped, a rubber band placed over the head can provide extra grip for the bit.

Maintenance Tips for Your Pocket Hole Jig

Maintaining your pocket hole jig ensures that it continues to function efficiently and accurately for many woodworking projects. Regular maintenance not only prolongs the life of the jig but also prevents common issues that can arise from wear and tear or improper use.

To begin with, always clean your pocket hole jig after each use. Remove wood chips and dust using a soft brush or compressed air. This prevents buildup that can clog the jig's components, particularly the drill guide holes. For a deeper clean, use a damp cloth to wipe down the jig, but avoid using harsh chemicals that might damage the metal or plastic parts.

Check the alignment of the drill guide periodically. Misalignment can result from regular use and can cause the drill bit to enter the wood at incorrect angles, compromising the strength of the joint. If you notice any misalignment, refer to the manufacturer's guidelines for adjustment procedures to ensure that everything is set correctly.

Lubrication is crucial for keeping the jig's moving parts functioning smoothly. Apply a dry lubricant to the drill guide bushings and any other moving components. This type of lubricant won't attract dust and debris, which could otherwise compound the problem by further clogging the system.

Inspect the drill bits regularly for signs of wear or damage. Dull or damaged drill bits can result in poor quality holes and difficult drilling, which can stress the jig and the material you are working with. Replace drill bits as soon as you notice signs of dulling or if the bit chips.

Keep an eye on the tightening mechanism, whether it's a knob, lever, or screw, used to secure the jig in place during use. These can become loose over time, which might lead to inaccuracies in drilling. Tighten these components as needed and check their integrity to ensure they hold the jig firmly.

For pocket hole jigs with adjustable settings for different wood thicknesses, ensure that these adjustments can be made smoothly. If you encounter resistance or if the settings do not hold as expected, this could be a sign that the adjustment mechanism needs cleaning or lubrication.

Storage is also an important aspect of maintaining your pocket hole jig. Store the jig in a cool, dry place to prevent rust and other damage caused by exposure to damp conditions. If the jig includes small parts or accessories, keep these together in a dedicated case or container to avoid loss and to keep everything organized for easy access.

When to Replace Parts

Replacing parts in a pocket hole jig is crucial for maintaining its performance and ensuring the accuracy and strength of your joinery. Knowing when to replace specific components can prevent project delays and the frustration of poor results.

One of the first signs that parts may need replacing is a noticeable decline in the quality of the drilled holes. If the holes become rough or irregular, it might be time to examine the drill bit and the guide bushings. The drill bit should be sharp and free of any nicks or wear. Over time, the cutting edges can dull, leading to less precise and clean cuts. When the bit no longer performs efficiently even after sharpening, it should be replaced.

Guide bushings also wear out with regular use. These components ensure the drill bit aligns correctly with the workpiece. Excessive play or visible scoring inside the bushing can misalign the drill bit, affecting the angle and depth of the pocket hole. Inspect bushings for signs of wear or deformation and replace them if they show any irregularities.

Another part to check regularly is the clamp. A pocket hole jig often includes an integrated clamp to hold the workpiece securely during drilling. If the clamp fails to hold the workpiece steadily, check its adjusting mechanism and the pad that contacts the wood. Worn or damaged pads can slip or mar the surface of the wood. Replacing the pad or the entire clamp mechanism might be necessary if tightening adjustments no longer maintain a firm hold.

Screws and fasteners within the jig itself should also be checked periodically. Loose or worn screws can affect the jig's stability and alignment. Tighten all screws regularly, and replace them if they are stripped or corroded.

Finally, for those who use their jigs frequently or in a professional capacity, keeping spare parts on hand can significantly reduce downtime. Having extra drill bits, bushings, and clamp pads makes it easy to swap out worn parts immediately, maintaining the continuity and efficiency of your work.

CHAPTER 9

Finishing Your Projects

Sanding and Preparing Joints for Finishing

Sanding and preparing joints for finishing are crucial steps in the woodworking process, especially when using a pocket hole jig. These steps ensure that the final product is smooth and aesthetically pleasing, while also preparing the surface for any stains or finishes to adhere properly.

When you begin sanding a project that includes pocket hole joints, it's important to start with a coarse grit sandpaper to remove any glue residue and to smooth out rough areas around the joints. Typically, starting with a 100-grit sandpaper works well. It's essential to sand in the direction of the wood grain to avoid creating scratches across the grain, which are difficult to remove later.

After the initial coarse sanding, progressively move to finer grits, such as 150-grit and then 220-grit, to create a smooth finish. This gradual progression helps in removing the scratches from the previous coarser grit, which is essential for a professional-quality finish. For pocket hole joints, pay extra attention to the areas around the holes. Even if you've used plugs to cover the holes, these areas may require additional sanding to ensure that the surface is uniform.

In addition to sanding, it's also important to thoroughly clean the wood after sanding and before applying any finish. This can be done using a tack cloth, which will pick up any remaining sawdust and debris. Ensuring that the surface is clean prevents imperfections in the finish and helps the stain or paint adhere better.

Once the wood is sanded and cleaned, applying a pre-stain wood conditioner is a good practice, especially for softer woods that tend to absorb stain unevenly. This conditioner helps to achieve a more even finish and reduces blotchiness.

After the conditioner has set, you can begin to apply your chosen finish, whether it's a stain, paint, or sealant. Each coat should be applied thinly and evenly, following the manufacturer's recommendations for drying times between coats. In between coats, a light sanding with very fine sandpaper (320-grit or higher) is recommended to remove any raised grain or dust nibs that have settled on the surface. This not only helps the subsequent coats adhere better but also contributes to an overall smoother finish.

The final step is often applying a protective topcoat, such as polyurethane, to safeguard the wood and the finish against wear and tear. This topcoat should be applied using a clean, high-quality brush or a spray system to achieve an even layer without drips or brush marks

Recommended Stains and Finishes

Choosing the right stains and finishes for your woodworking projects that utilize pocket hole joinery is crucial for both aesthetic appeal and long-term durability. The type of wood, the intended use of the piece, and the environmental conditions it will face are all important factors to consider.

For projects involving softwoods like pine or cedar, which are commonly used with pocket hole jigs, a pre-stain wood conditioner is recommended. This helps to prevent blotches by promoting a more uniform absorption of the stain. When selecting a stain, oil-based stains are often preferred for their depth of color and long-lasting protection. They penetrate deeply into the wood, enhancing its natural grain. However, they require a longer drying time, which can be a consideration if the project timeline is tight.

Water-based stains are another option, especially for those who prefer a quicker drying time and easier cleanup. These stains are less likely to emit strong odors and VOCs (Volatile Organic Compounds), making them a safer choice for indoor projects. Although they do not penetrate as deeply as oil-based stains, they come in a wide variety of colors and can be built up in layers to achieve the desired intensity.

After staining, applying a finish will protect the wood from wear, moisture, and other environmental factors.

Polyurethane is a popular choice for projects that require a durable finish. It is available in both oil-based and water-based forms. Oil-based polyurethane offers a more durable finish with a warmer, amber hue that can enhance the depth and richness of wood grain. However, it has a longer drying time and a stronger odor. Water-based polyurethane dries quickly and remains clear, preserving the original color of the stain beneath, but it may not be as durable as its oil-based counterpart.

For items that will come into contact with food, such as dining tables or kitchen cabinets, consider a food-safe finish like a butcher block conditioner or mineral oil. These products protect the wood while ensuring it is safe to come into contact with food items.

For outdoor projects, a spar urethane is recommended due to its resistance to water and UV damage, which helps prevent the wood from warping, cracking, or fading. This is particularly important for items like outdoor furniture or garden structures made using pocket hole joinery.

Finally, for those who prefer a natural look, finishing waxes or oils, such as linseed or tung oil, can be used. These products provide a softer finish that may need to be reapplied periodically but will deeply penetrate and nourish the wood, enhancing its natural beauty and feel.

Final Assembly and Presentation

Final assembly and presentation are crucial stages in woodworking, where the craftsmanship of earlier steps comes to fruition and the true quality of the work is revealed. When using a pocket hole jig, these phases are particularly important because they highlight the strength and subtlety of the joints involved.

After all pocket holes have been drilled and components are joined, the first task in final assembly is to ensure all joints are tight and well-aligned. This often involves a final round of clamping and adjustment to prevent any shifts that might have occurred during the joining process. It's important to double-check that all screws are snug and that no parts of the joint protrude or misalign, as these can affect the final appearance and functionality of the piece.

Once the structure is solidified, the next step is to address any pocket holes that remain visible. Many woodworkers choose to use pocket hole plugs to fill these gaps. Selecting the right wood species and grain pattern for the plugs can make them blend seamlessly with the surrounding material. For best results, glue the plugs in place, let them dry, and then trim or sand them down flush with the surface. This not only enhances the aesthetics but also adds to the integrity of the finished piece.

Sanding the entire project is essential, not just where the plugs were inserted but also along all surfaces and edges. Starting with a coarser grit to remove any glue residue or rough spots, and progressing to finer grits, creates a smooth, professional finish. Sanding is not just about aesthetics; it also prepares the wood for staining or painting by opening up the pores of the timber.

When choosing a finish, consider both the type of wood and the intended use of the piece. Stains can accentuate the natural beauty of the wood, while paints can add a bold or complementary color to the décor. Applying a clear coat over paint or stain can protect the surface from wear and tear and enhance the depth and richness of the finish. It is crucial to apply these finishes evenly and allow adequate drying time between coats as recommended by the manufacturer.

The final presentation should focus on the overall look and functionality of the piece. This is the time to add any additional hardware, like knobs or handles, that complement the design. Ensuring that these final touches are both functional and aesthetically pleasing will reflect the quality and care taken throughout the woodworking process.

CHAPTER 10

Project Ideas and Inspiration

Beginner Projects to Get Started

When starting with a pocket hole jig, it's essential to choose projects that will build your confidence and skills gradually. One of the best projects for a beginner is a simple wooden step stool. This project teaches the basics of measuring, cutting, and joining pieces using a pocket hole jig. The stool requires minimal materials—usually just a few boards—and the end product is both functional and gratifying.

Another excellent project for newcomers is a basic picture frame. This project introduces more precise measuring and cutting, requiring accuracy for a clean finish. By using the pocket hole jig, beginners learn how to create strong, hidden joints that are more aesthetically pleasing than external screws or nails. The simplicity of a picture frame makes it a quick project with very useful results, perfect for practicing new skills.

Building a wooden planter box is another great beginner project. This introduces working with larger pieces of wood while still being a manageable size for new woodworkers. The planter box project focuses on constructing a box shape, which is fundamental in many woodworking projects. It also offers an opportunity to explore outdoor finishes and woods that are more resistant to weather.

For those interested in furniture, constructing a simple coffee table can be an ambitious yet achievable project. A basic rectangular coffee table provides a larger canvas to practice the skills learned from smaller projects. It often involves creating a tabletop, legs, and maybe a bottom shelf. This project will reinforce lessons in stability and weight distribution, which are crucial for building larger pieces in the future.

Lastly, a wall shelf is a functional project that teaches both joinery and the nuances of mounting finished projects securely on a wall. Wall shelves can be as simple or complex as one desires, but even the simplest designs require precision to ensure they are level and sturdy when mounted. This project allows beginners to experiment with different styles and finishes, adding a personal touch to their creations.

Intermediate Projects to Enhance Skills

Intermediate woodworking projects are an excellent way for enthusiasts to enhance their skills using a pocket hole jig. One such project is the construction of a sturdy, stylish coffee table that incorporates storage solutions. To begin, select high-quality hardwood like oak or maple for a durable finish. Cut the wood into pieces for the top, bottom, and sides of the table. Use the pocket hole jig to drill angled holes that will allow for the pieces to be joined discreetly and securely with screws, avoiding visible joint lines and maintaining a clean aesthetic.

Another great project is a wall-mounted shelving unit, which involves creating multiple shelves of varying lengths to add a dynamic look to any room. The pocket hole jig is used to attach the shelves to the wall studs as well as to connect the individual shelf supports. This technique ensures that the screws are hidden and the unit looks professionally made. It's important to measure the spacing between shelves carefully to accommodate items of different sizes.

Building a wooden bench with a flip-top seat offers both seating and storage, perfect for entryways or mudrooms. Begin by constructing a box frame and then use the pocket hole jig to attach legs and the bench top. The flip-top should be attached with hinges and designed to open easily for storing shoes, hats, or other outdoor essentials. This project not only refines the use of the jig in creating functional furniture but also in implementing hardware like hinges.

A more challenging project could be creating a farmhouse-style dining chair. This involves crafting a frame from hardwood, using the jig to assemble the back, seat, and legs. The back should be slightly angled for comfort, and the seat can be either wood or upholstered, depending on preference. This project tests precision in creating more complex furniture pieces that must be both aesthetically pleasing and structurally sound.

Advanced Projects for Mastering Pocket Hole Joinery

Mastering pocket hole joinery opens up a realm of possibilities for creating complex and durable woodworking projects. Experienced woodworkers who have honed their skills on basic and intermediate projects can take their craft to the next level by undertaking advanced projects that challenge their precision and ingenuity.

One sophisticated project to consider is building a custom entertainment center. This large-scale project not only serves as a focal point in a living room but also provides ample opportunity to practice and perfect pocket hole joinery. The entertainment center can be designed with adjustable shelving, hidden compartments for electronics, and intricate door panels. Using pocket holes for this project ensures strong, seamless joints that are crucial for the heavy load of electronic devices and regular usage.

Another challenging project is a dining room table with removable leaves. This allows the table to be versatile and adaptable to different group sizes. The use of pocket holes makes the table's assembly and disassembly straightforward, with secure locking mechanisms that can be easily hidden from view. The key challenge here is ensuring that all pieces align perfectly when assembled to maintain a smooth, uniform tabletop.

For those interested in outdoor furniture, constructing a set of Adirondack chairs can be both rewarding and demanding. These chairs require careful attention to the angle of the backrest and seat to ensure comfort. Pocket hole joinery is ideal for these angles because it provides strong joints that can withstand weather conditions if the right type of treated wood and proper sealants are used.

A rolling kitchen island is a functional project that involves creating a movable piece with a solid worktop and storage options below. This project tests a woodworker's ability to integrate casters that can handle weight and frequent movement. Using pocket holes for attaching shelves and side panels provides the durability needed for a kitchen environment where the island will be subjected to various loads and uses.

Lastly, building a Murphy bed presents an advanced challenge that requires precision and careful planning. The bed must be perfectly balanced to ensure it folds up and down smoothly, and the frame must be securely attached to the wall. Pocket holes are used extensively in the cabinet and frame construction to create tight joints that are essential for the folding mechanism to operate correctly.

CHAPTER 11

Conclusion

Throughout the exploration of the pocket hole jig, it becomes evident that this simple tool is invaluable for any woodworker looking to enhance their craftsmanship. The versatility of the pocket hole jig allows for a wide range of applications, from basic repairs to intricate furniture designs, making it a staple in any woodworking workshop.

The key strength of pocket hole joinery lies in its ability to create strong, durable joints quickly and easily without the need for complex clamping setups or specialized skills. This makes it an excellent choice for both beginners and seasoned professionals. Additionally, the clean finish provided by pocket hole joinery, with screws hidden away, ensures that projects not only hold up over time but also have a sleek, professional appearance.

By mastering the use of a pocket hole jig, woodworkers can significantly cut down on project time and increase efficiency. The ability to work faster without sacrificing quality allows for more projects to be completed, and it opens up the opportunity to tackle more complex builds that might have seemed daunting before.

As demonstrated in the various projects and techniques discussed, from simple joinery on straightforward projects to more complex applications like furniture and cabinetry, the pocket hole jig is adaptable. Its use in both functional and decorative aspects of woodworking showcases its breadth of utility.

Made in the USA
Middletown, DE
10 June 2025

76799877R00046